Hello there I am busy writing my second book in the
Lost Cartoon series

Unfortunately at the moment not much has been
scanned however In time it too will be complete.

What you are about to see is my later work that
eventually led to my fiction that you read and hopefully
enjoy today.

So begins our journey through 1997 to 2006.

What the next few consist of is dreams that I had that
became what you see below however as to an actual
cartoon they haven't been created yet.

I hope by the end to include cartoon versions even now.

Bugs Bunnies Brigade

N.: "Ah Spring."

"the wonderful colorful birds, (chirp, chirp) the ("desert") American bald eagle, (over lake) (american flag under right wing) and what's that over there? (mountain snow) Oh I get it it's our pal Bugs Bunny."

(go to close up)

"Eh, What's up doc?"

Bugs: "Hey, where is everybody?!"

Narrator: "Say! That's a good idea. Let's find out."

(go to closure)

Elmer: "I'm hunting ducks, its duck season, Ho, hu, hu, hu,

Daffy: "Well I can't understand why Fuddy Duddy because its really Rabbit Season!"

(says three times)
Elmer: x "Its Duck
Season" x ↓ x ↓ x (says three times)
Daffy "x Wabbit Season")
(Bugs steps in whispering "Wabbit Season")
Elmer "Wabbit Season"

Daffy "Duck Season"!

Elmer "Wabbit Season"

Daffy "I say its
Duck Season, and I say "fire!"

Bam! Daffy's
bill is shot upwards,

* Daffy picks
it up and says
to Bugs "your
despicable"

Bugs says
"Wow look!"
Elmer does
"A Jackalope!"
Daffy says "Where?"
Bugs says "Right here!"
pointing at Daffy
Daffy says "Hah Hah, Hah,
that's rich a DB say!"
Elmer sees the sign

Daffy uh, oh,
Bang! el

feathers all roughed
out look like
a lion.
elmer lowers gun, Daffy

moves towards Bugs,
Daffy "your
despicable!"

Bugs "So you
are for a crab,
Daffy What! I'm a
crab. I'm a
crab?" Elmer looks
Crab season

Daffy "Not again,
Bang

Daffy in
dissevaled mess
says (to Bugs) ha, ha, it is
to laugh. y Bugs shrugs
Daffy turns jumps up
over towards Elmer
~~Daffy~~ ~~Bugs~~ No you Idiot it's
Duck Season not
crab!
Elmer "oh... huh,
huh, huh, huh, huh"

Bugs B. has changed
sign,

Daffy: ~~It~~ ~~Ra Duck~~ reads sign
Season!?

Elmer: ~~season~~ It is
oh boy!))

Daffy: "Not again"
tries to ~~close~~ cover
mouth with hand
but doesn't in
time,

Bang!

Bugs: "Well so
long, got to
go!))

Elmer: "Hey come back here!" (sees burrowing)

Daffy: "Oh boy!" "Here's my chance." (jumps in hole)

Bugs: "I wonder where that crazy Duck is?"

(Daffy pops in)

Daffy: "Well I'm here! where ever here is."

Elmer (comes out of hole): "NOW I got you!"

Daffy:
"Oh No! not again!"
Bl-lam-m! Daffy
gets chased and
people run away
Elmer: "What
you screwy
duck!" Blam!
Blam! Blam!
Blam! Blam!

"Come back
here"

Daffy: "yah!"
more chasing
"Elmer: I'll get you yet!"
Bugs: "Ahh,
there's nothing
like the right
kind of intert-
ainment, I always

say."

[The End]

— Detective Daffy

Nov 2, 02
Jonathan Riccord

Plot Line

To avoid paying extra taxes Yosimite Sam is turned into Fudd by Witch Hazzel!

Daffy: "I'm one the scene my Porko friend!

Porky: "Oh sure"

Daffy: "He can't hide forever we'll find him if

my name isn't
detective duck.
They chase him
down with amusing
results.

It's similar to
the cop cartoon
except Sam
uses Witch Hazels
magic. At the
end the magic
sets Daffy on
fire and he
runs into Sam.

Last Scene - Police
Station

Daffy: "Well,
we never found
the Witch but we

found a
terrible pain."

He shows his tail
and the cartoon ends.

Before we go any further you'll probably be thinking what is a rabbit have to do with cartoons, well to make a long story short I once owned a rabbit named Flopsy and I had an idea to experiment with her to see if I could do a take off of Garfield with her as the main character.

Although the idea was cute Flopsy Adventures never got off the ground but it did lead to some interesting results.

In the process of this experimentation I created Smily the Worm and Ali the Red Gator.

I also decided to make Yum Yum a star.

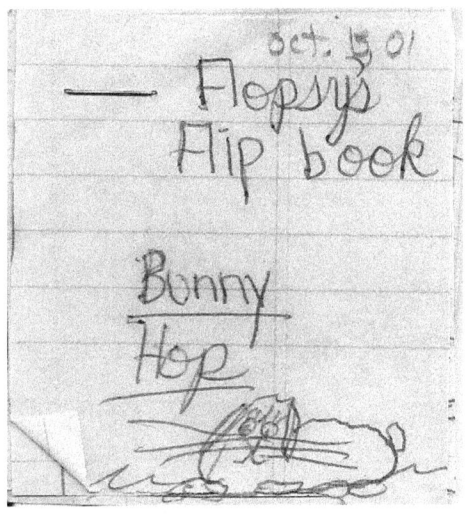

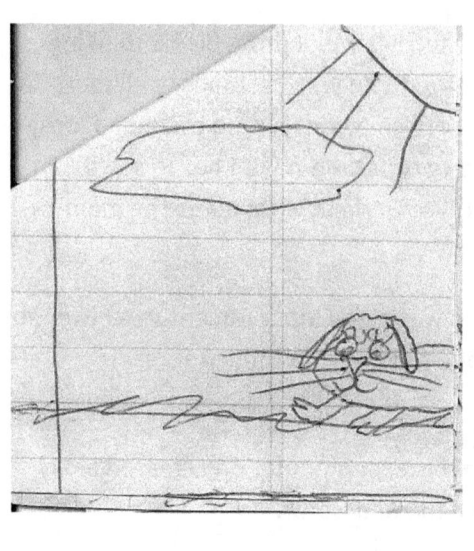

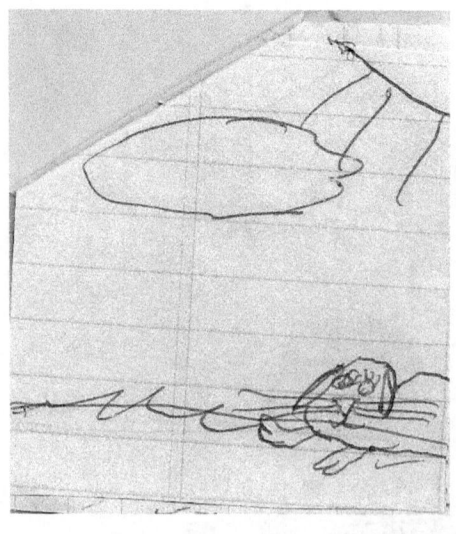

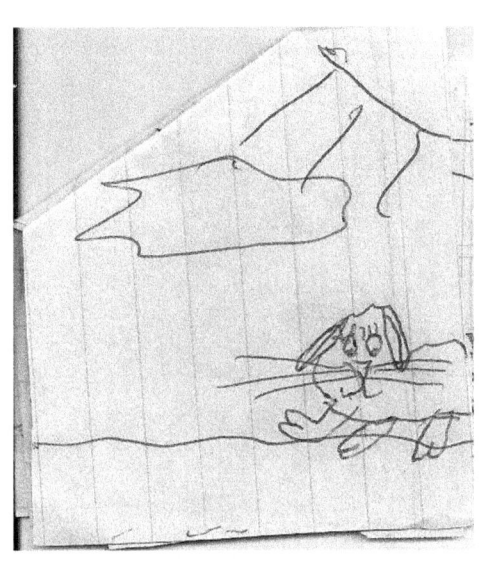

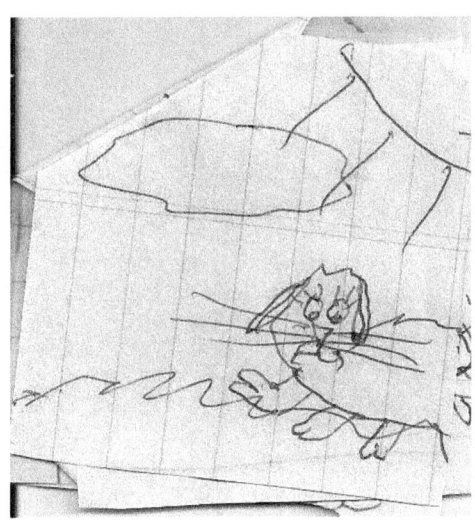

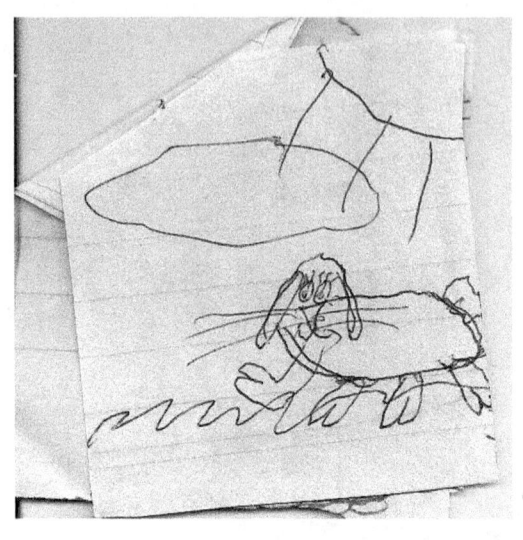

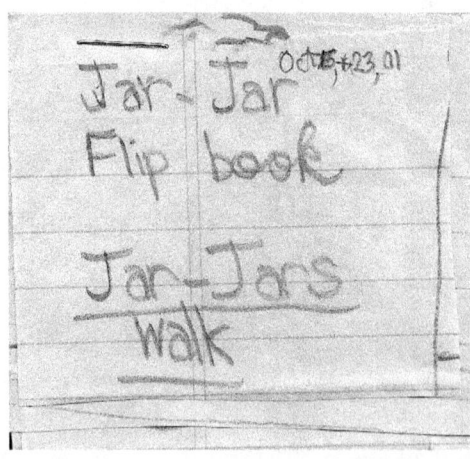

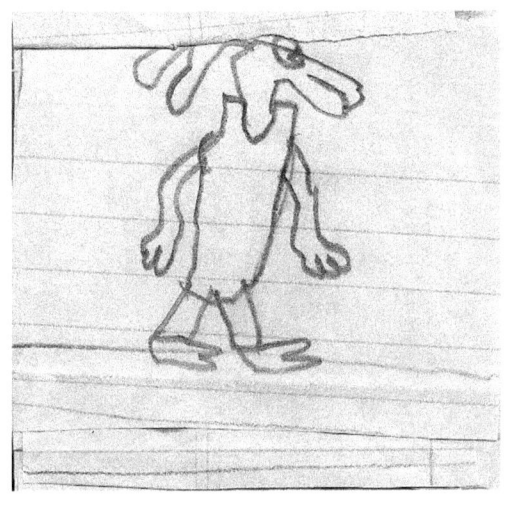

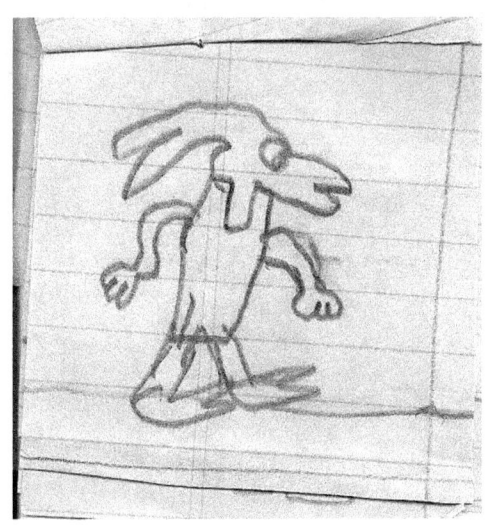

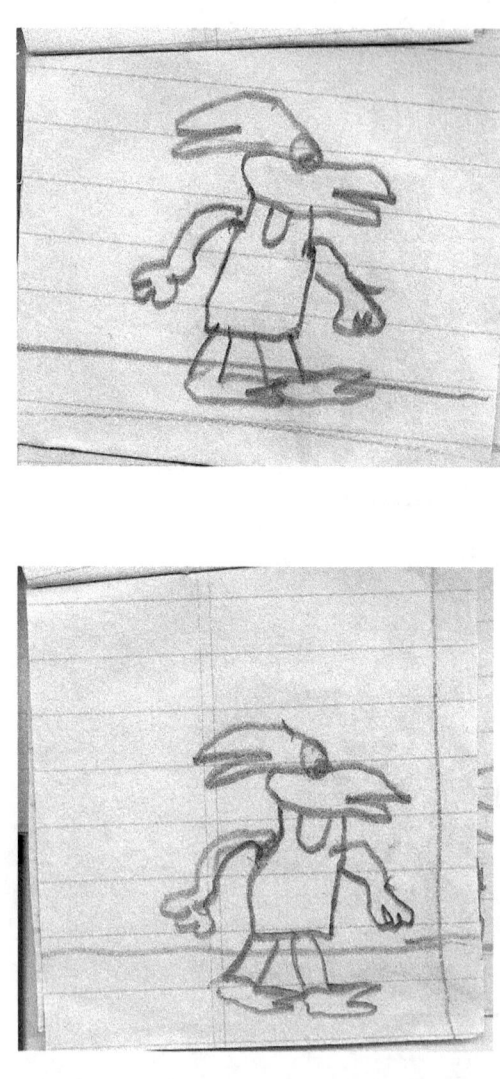

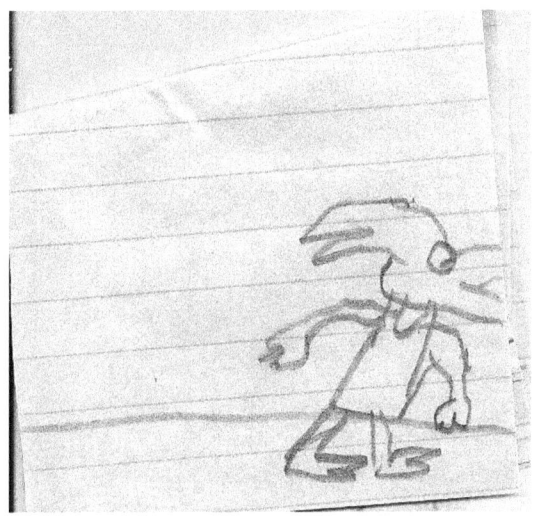

This next work was an idea I had to make Roadrunner comics as of old, by using my own ideas to create a feeling of nostalgia.

If most folks don't know the Roadrunner stared in a number of comics of his own called Beep Beep the Roadrunner.

I hope you enjoy seeing my interpatation.

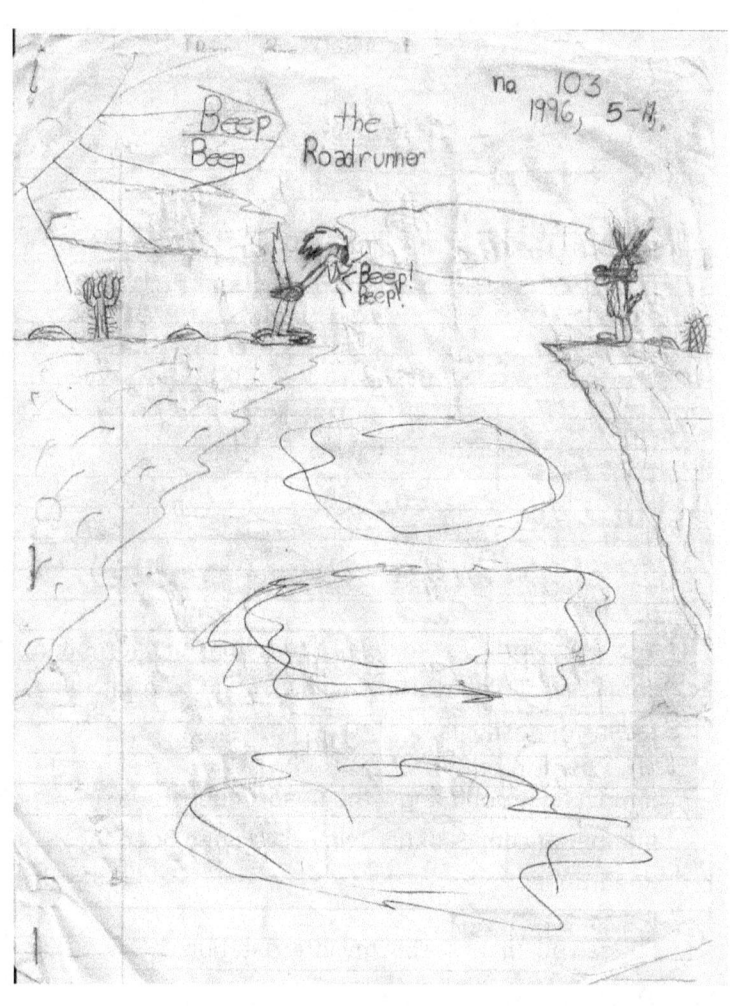

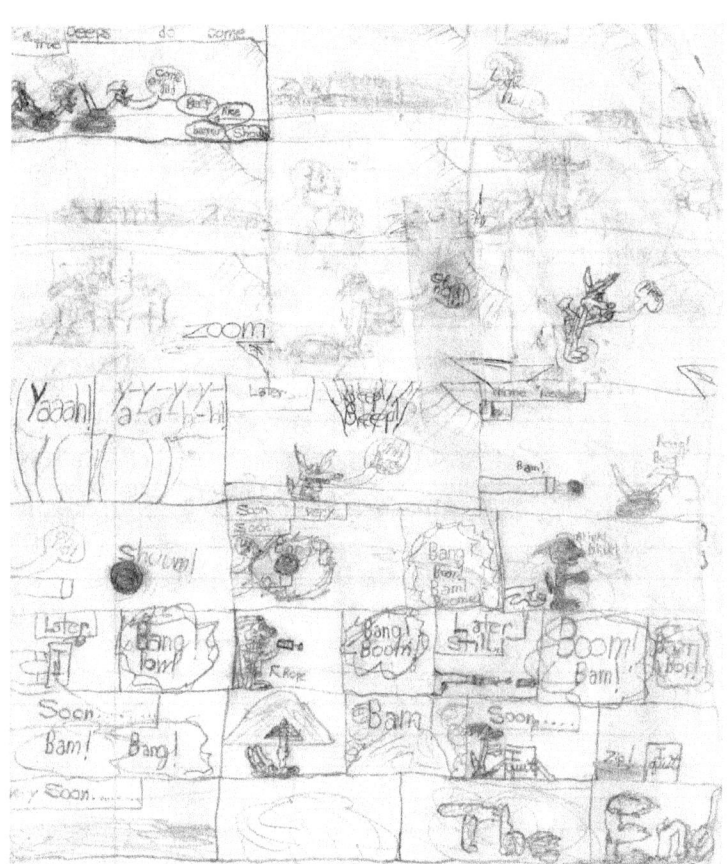

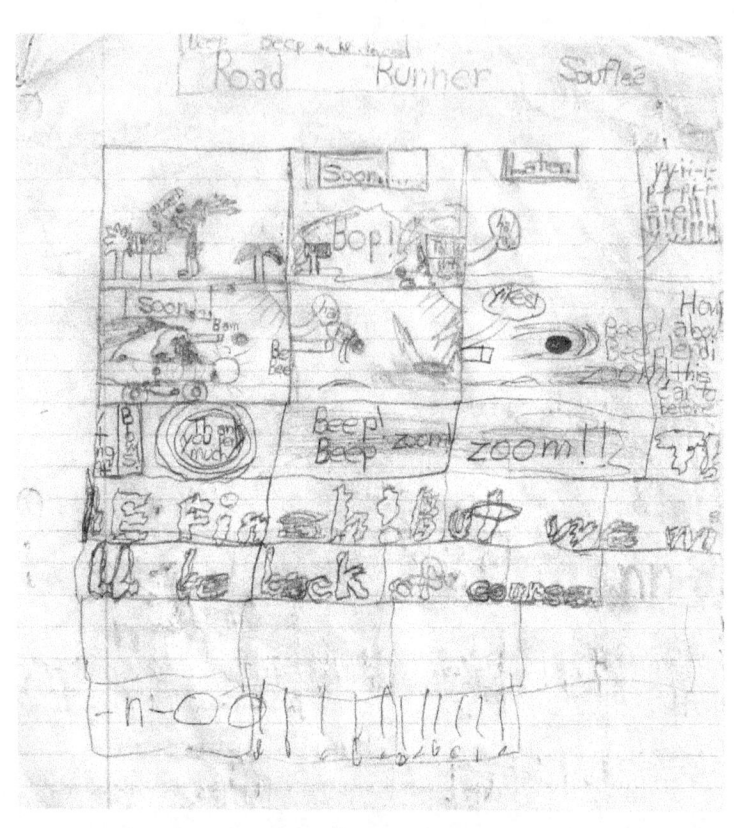

Beep   Beep
The   Roadrunner
no: 94   1996, 5-6,

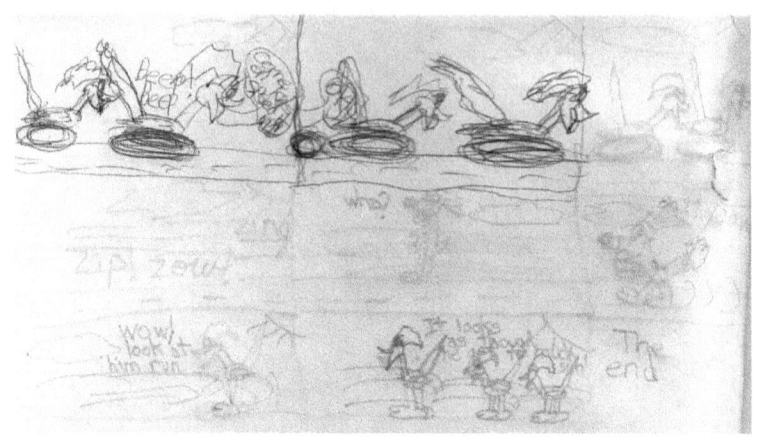

To be authentic to the series their was a copyright number thrown in but seeing that I didn't want trouble I took it out.

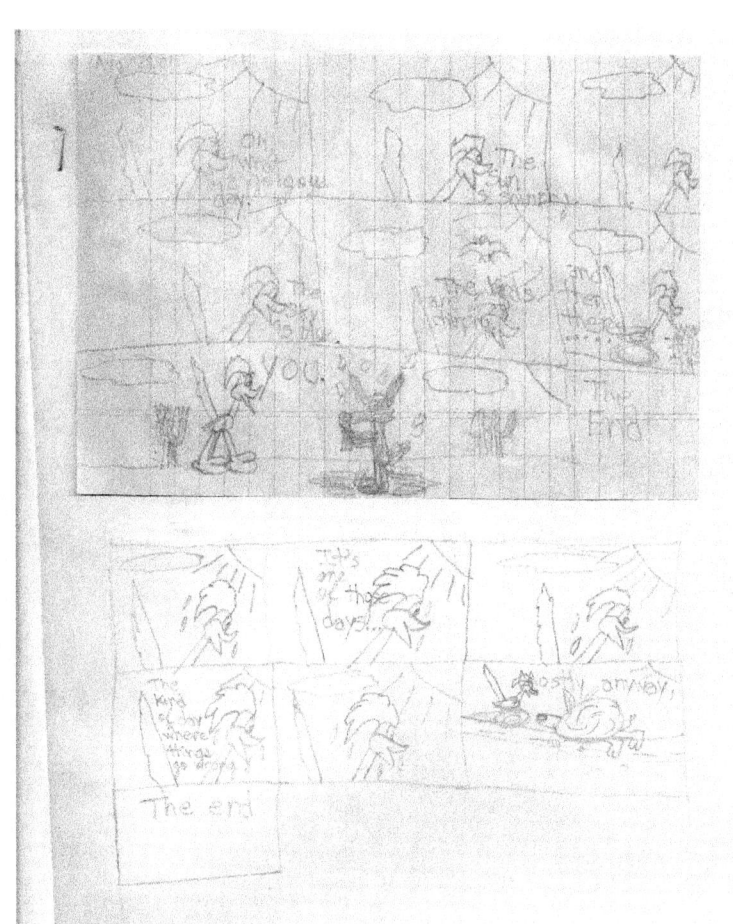

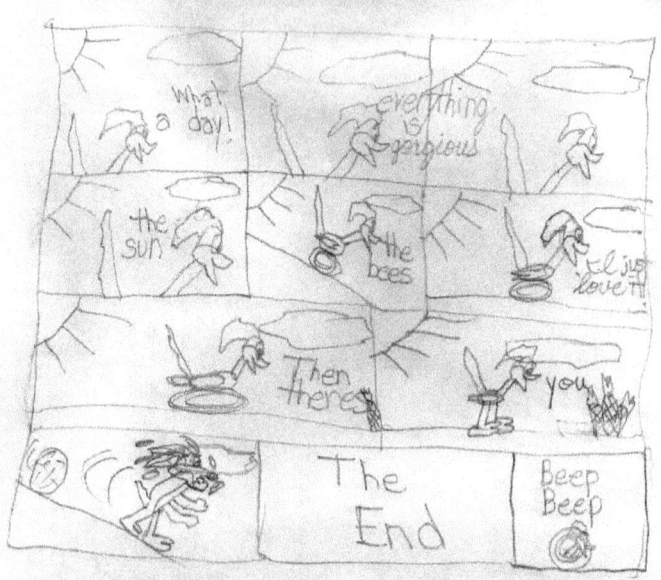

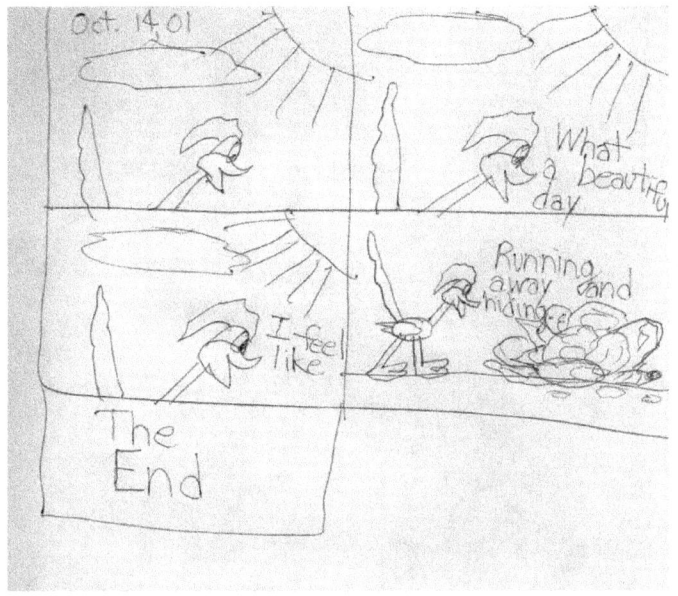

I believe the next one was done in Yellowstone however there is no date to clarify that account.

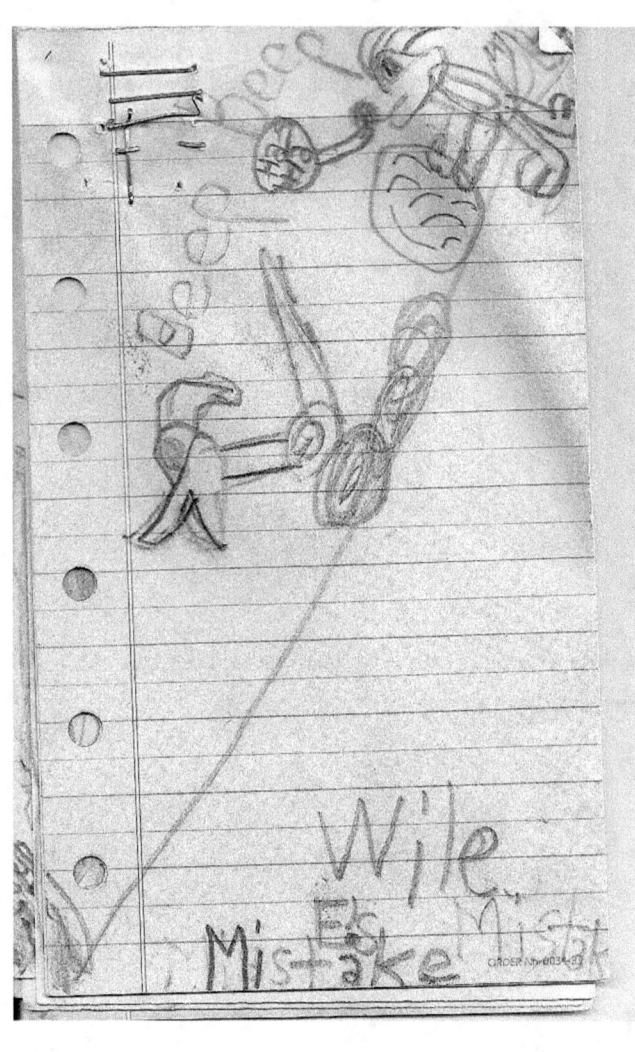

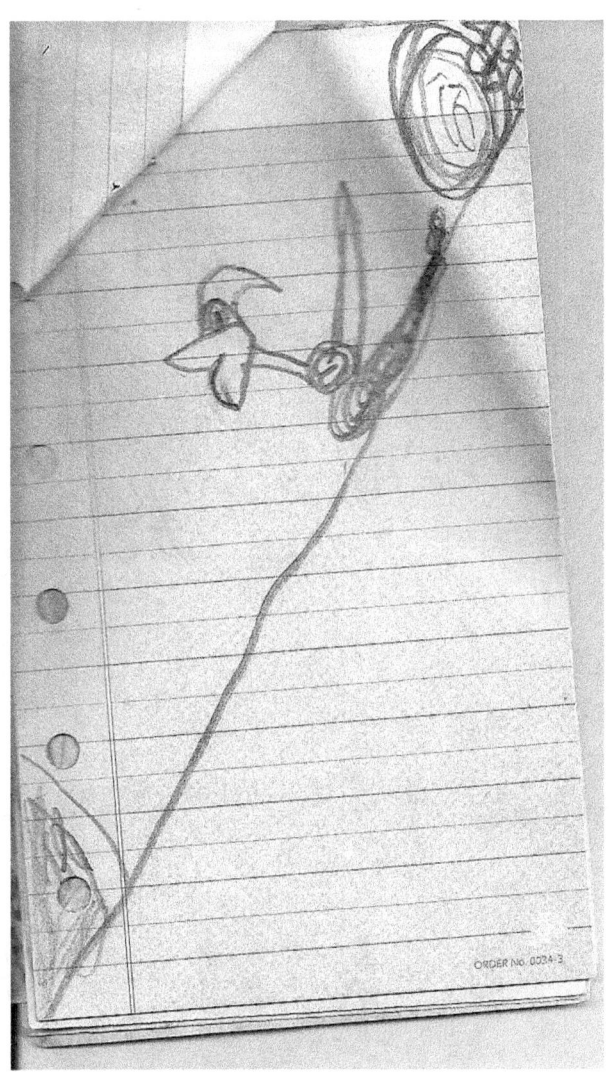

ORDER No. 0034-3

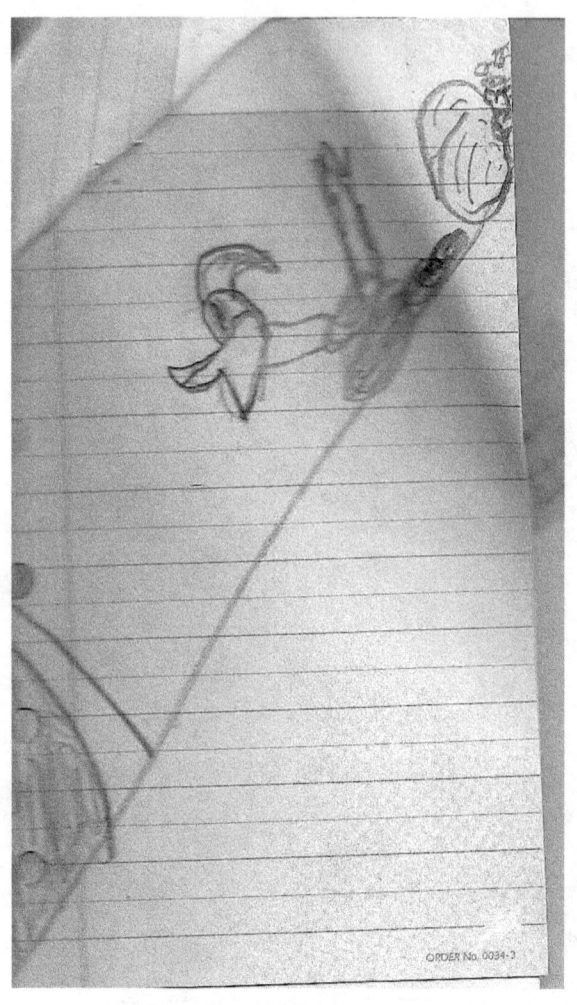

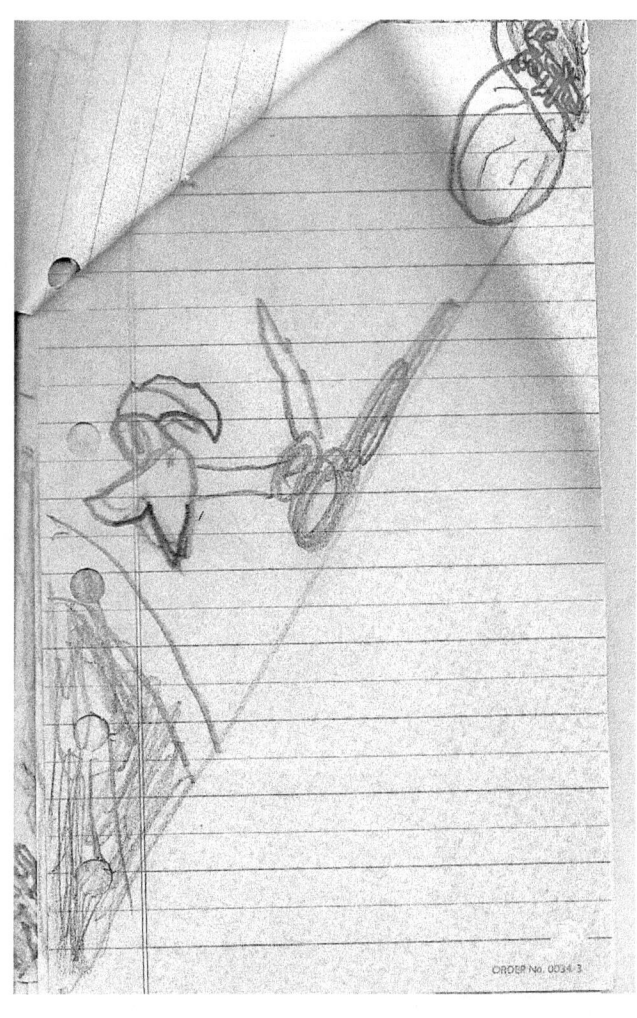

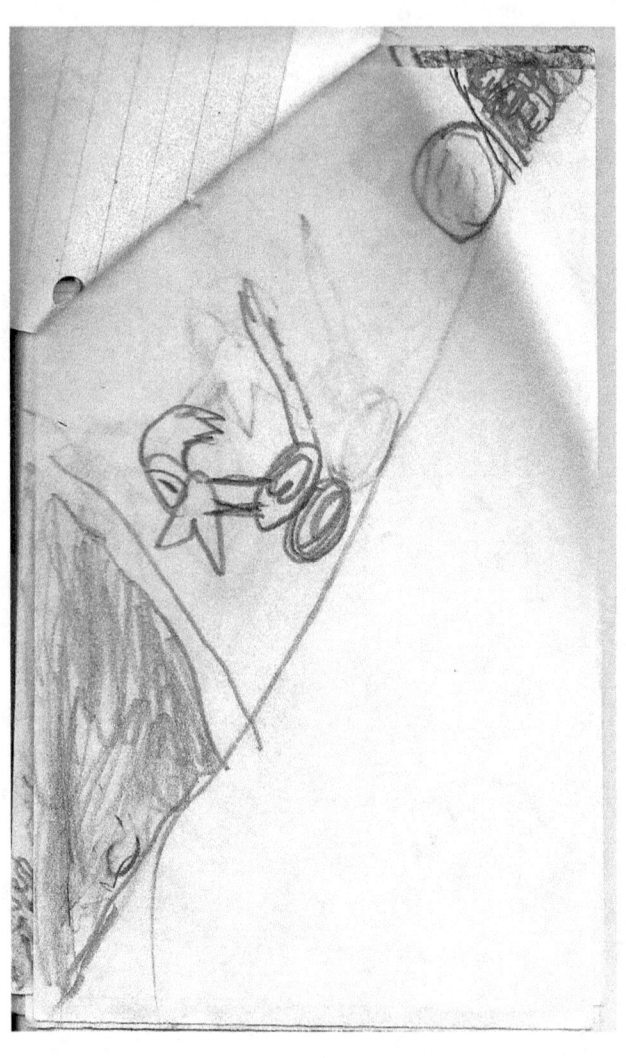

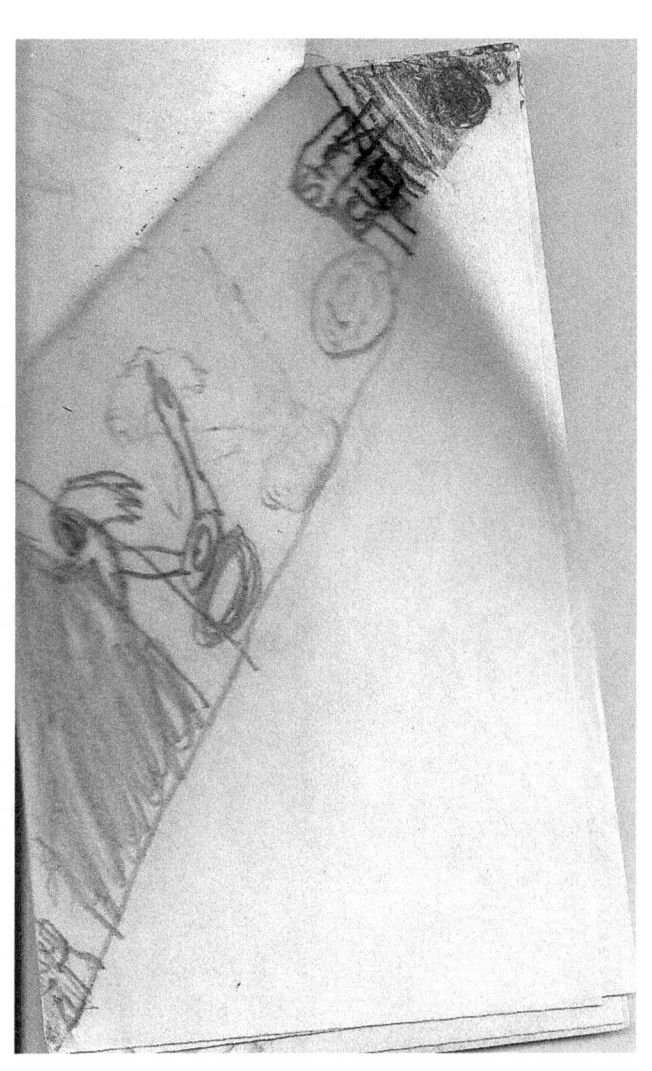

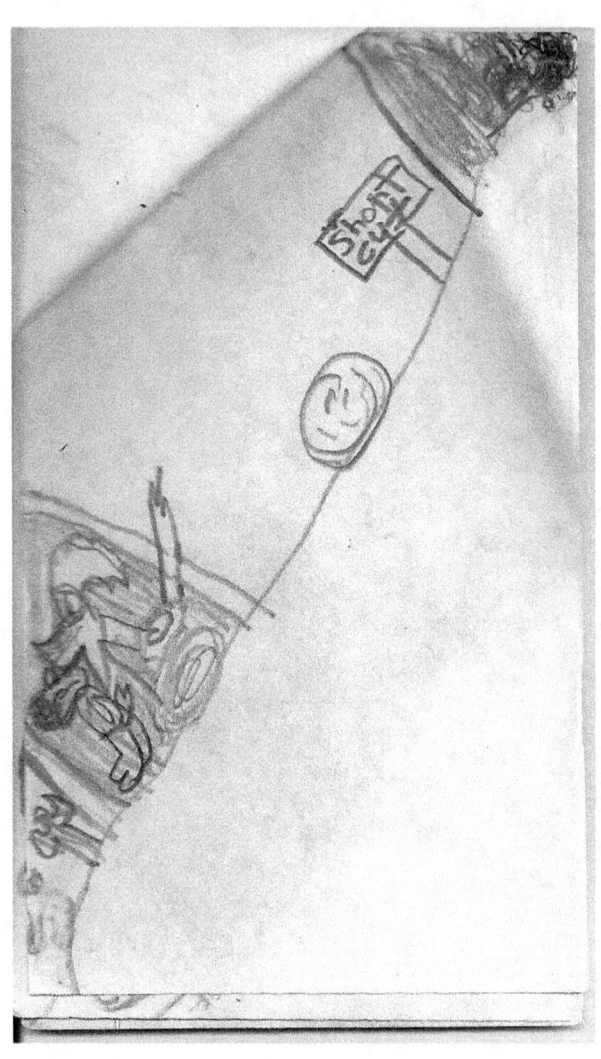

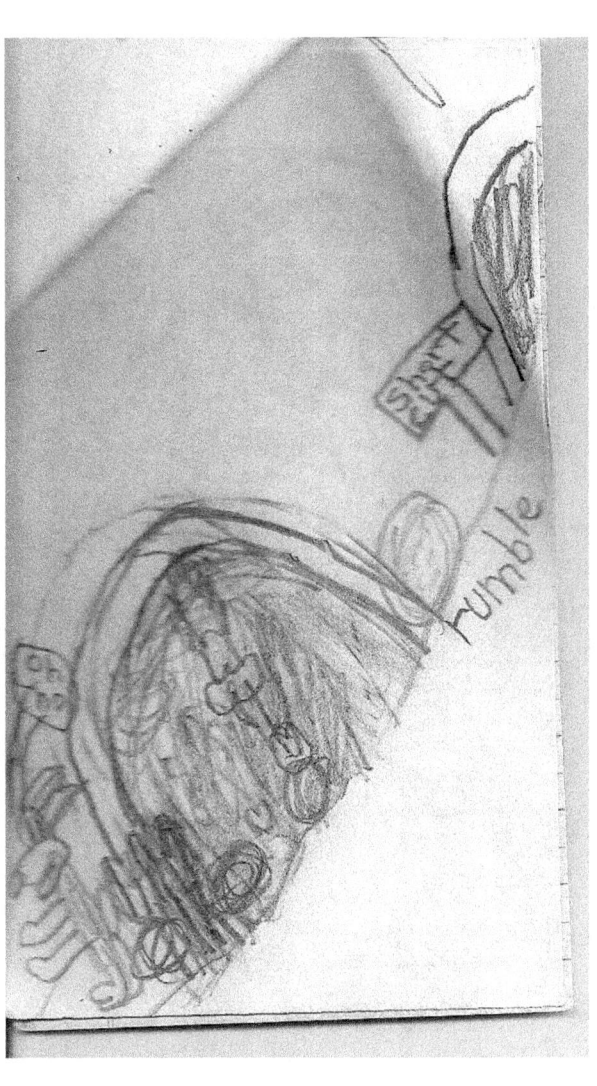

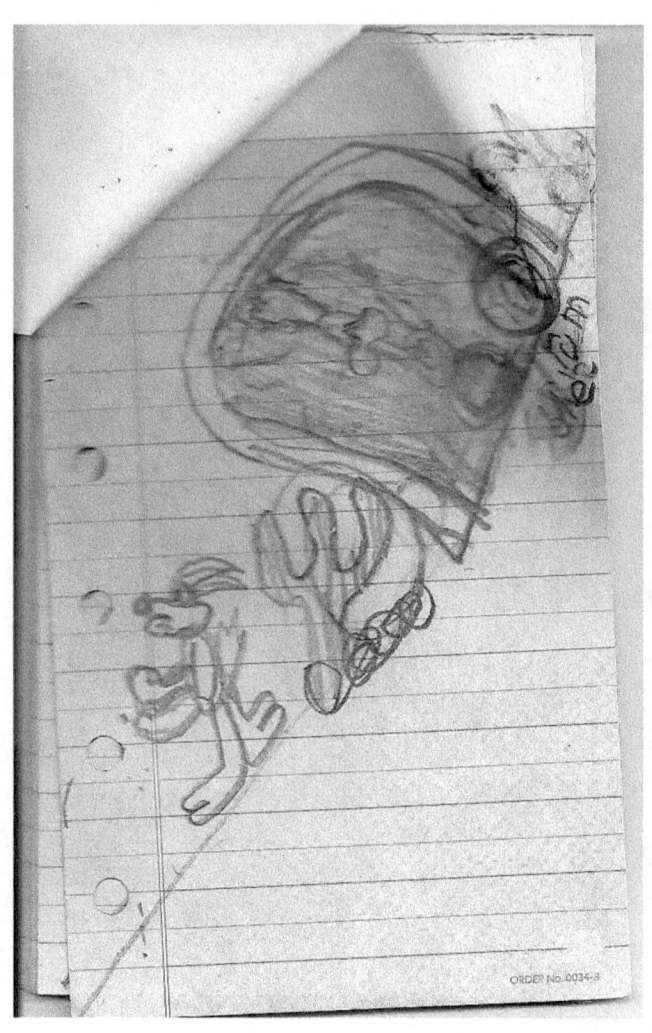

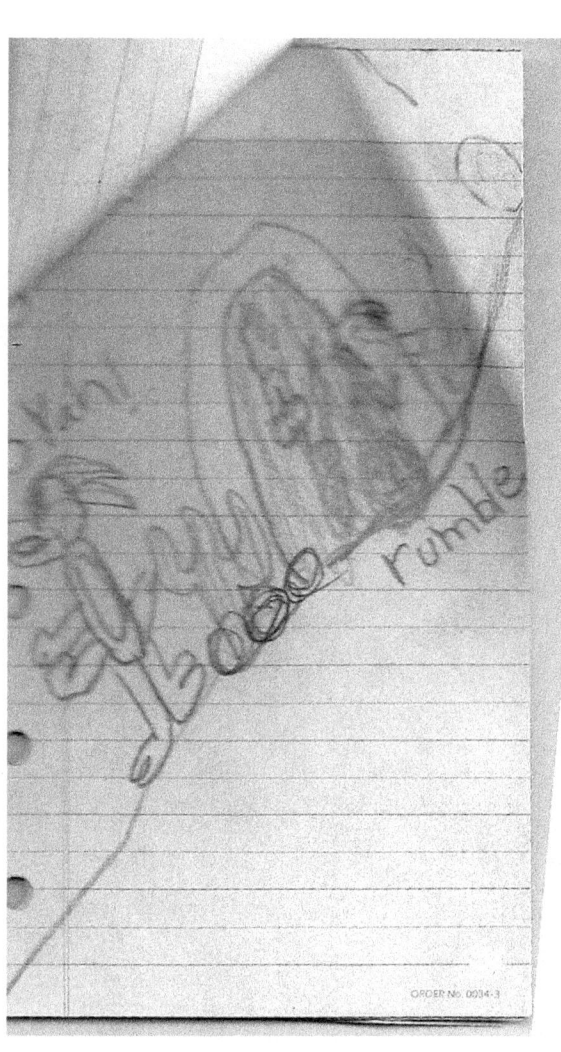

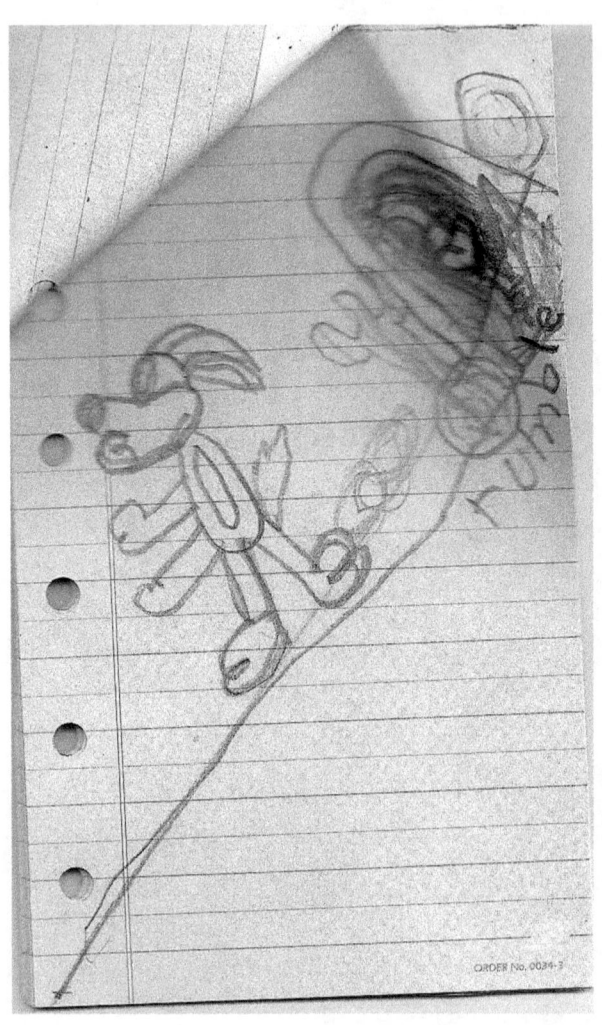

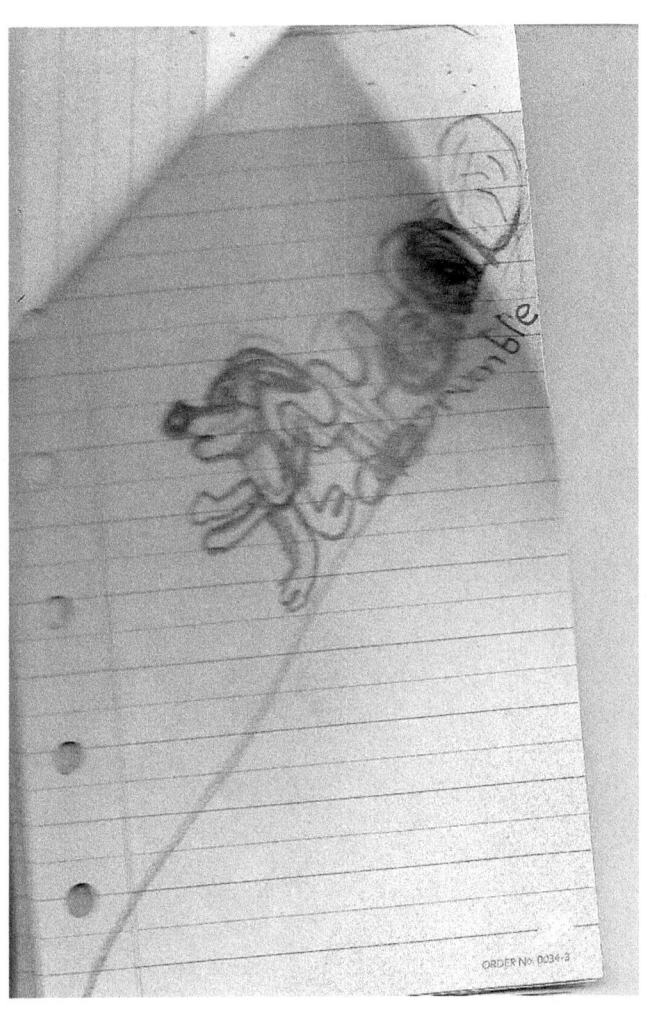

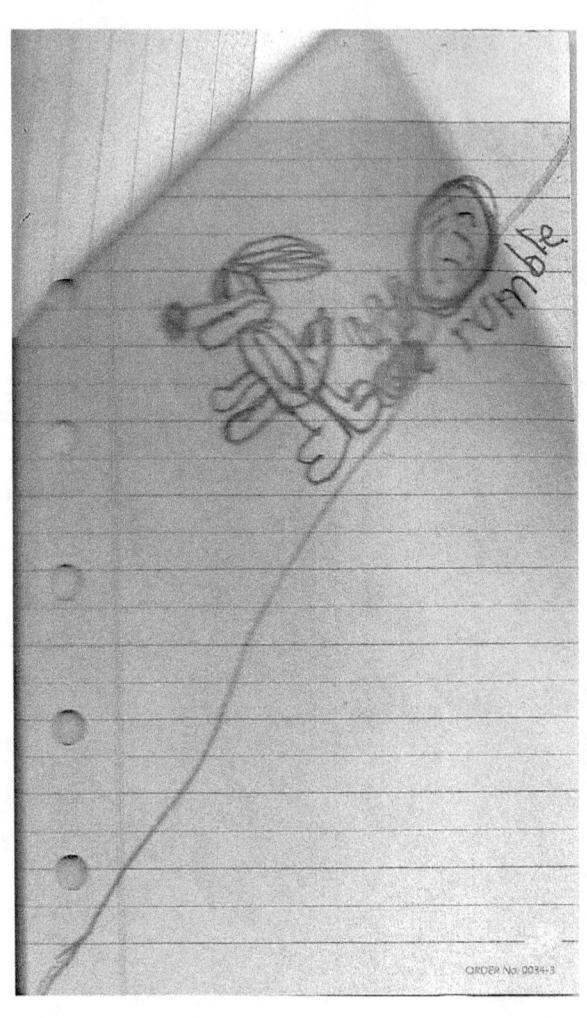

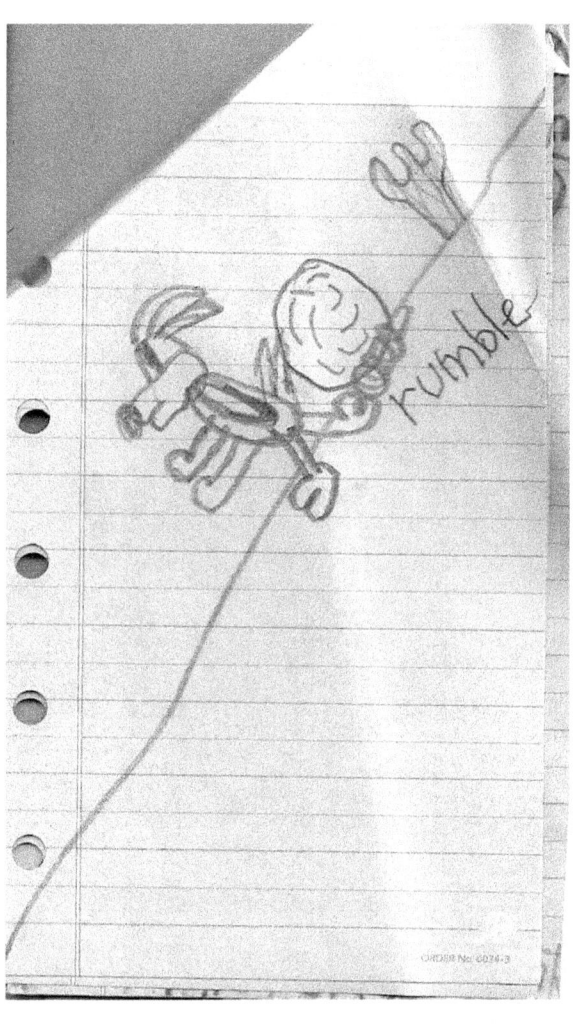

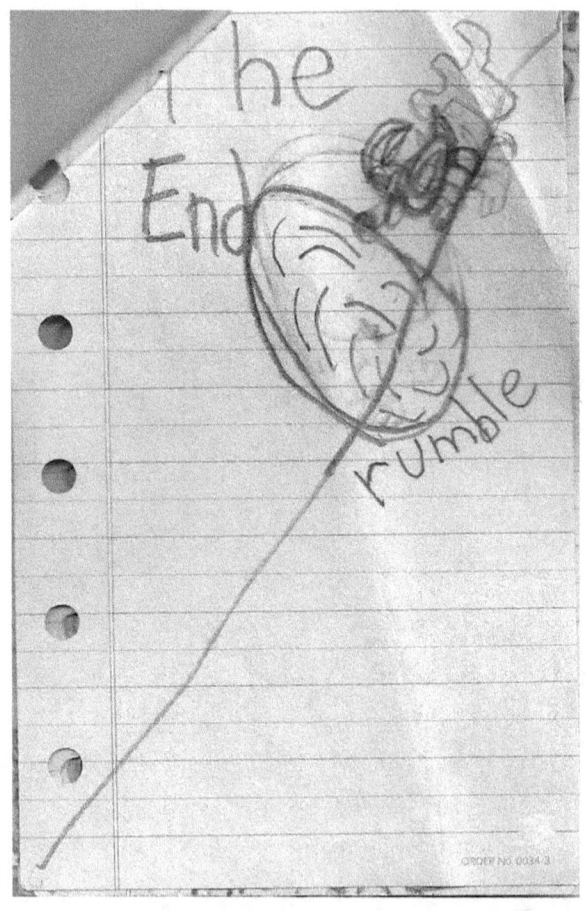

Obviously to me the shortcut idea came from the Roadrunner Pc game.

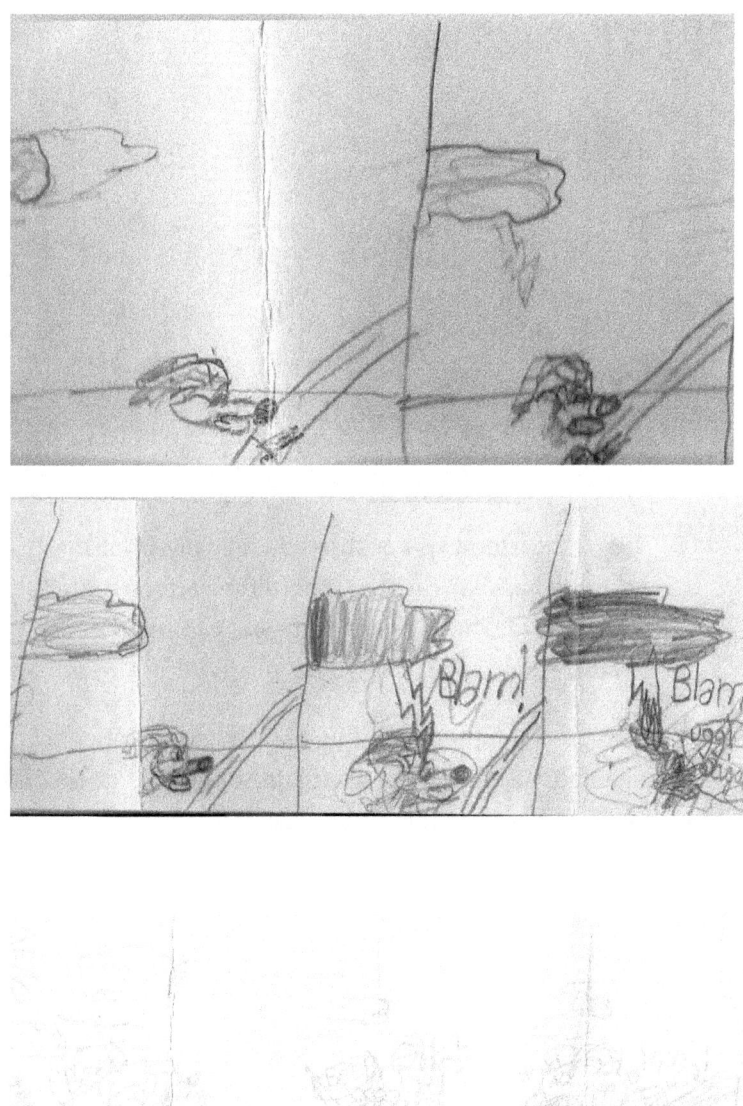

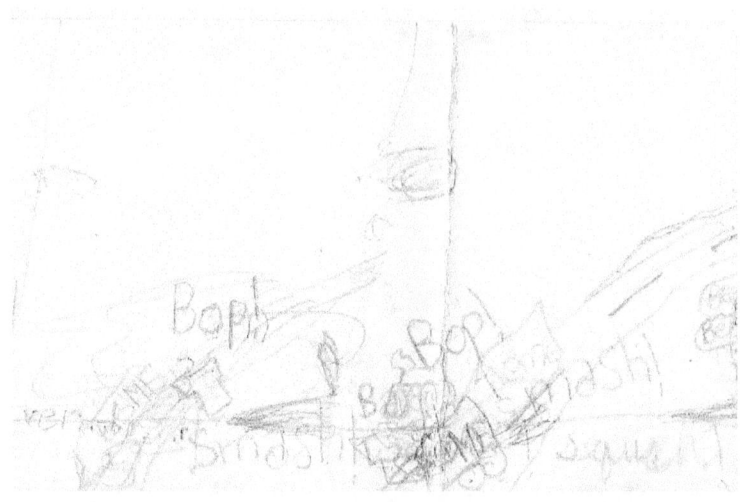

This next cartoon was destroyed originally I foolishly wrote on baseball card cardboard the cartoon and asked dad to scan it when I came back to see the results it was thrown away.

I panicked completely and finally after some thought I regained my memory of what I drew placed it down on paper and now people can see what it looks like.

Whew! What a relief!

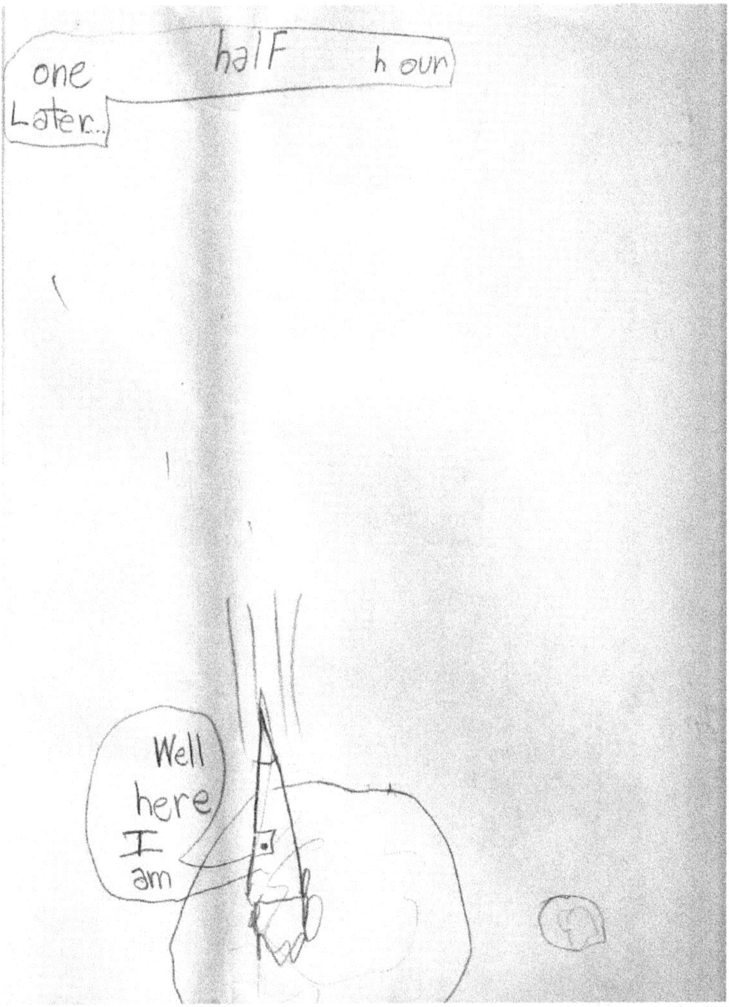
one half hour Later...
Well here I am

age 3

5 min.
Later....

good
Job

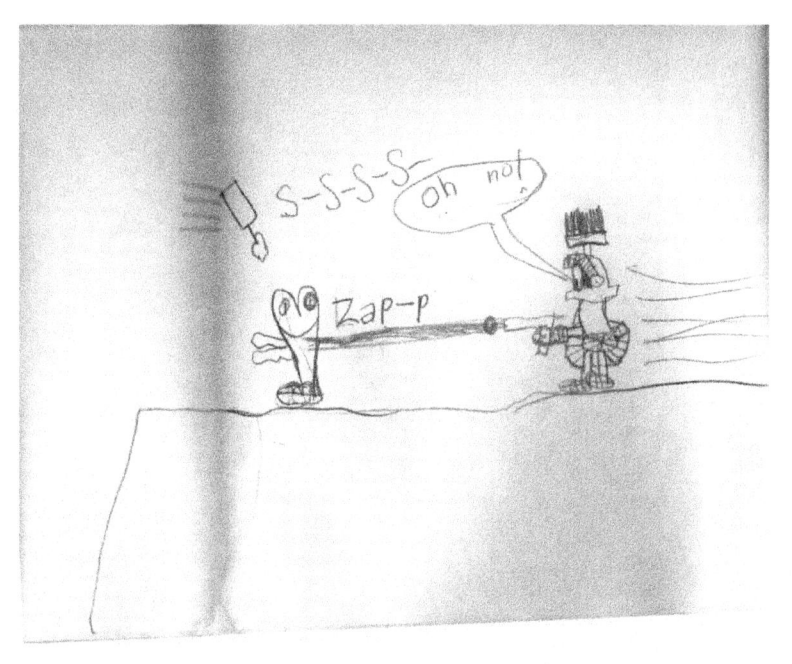

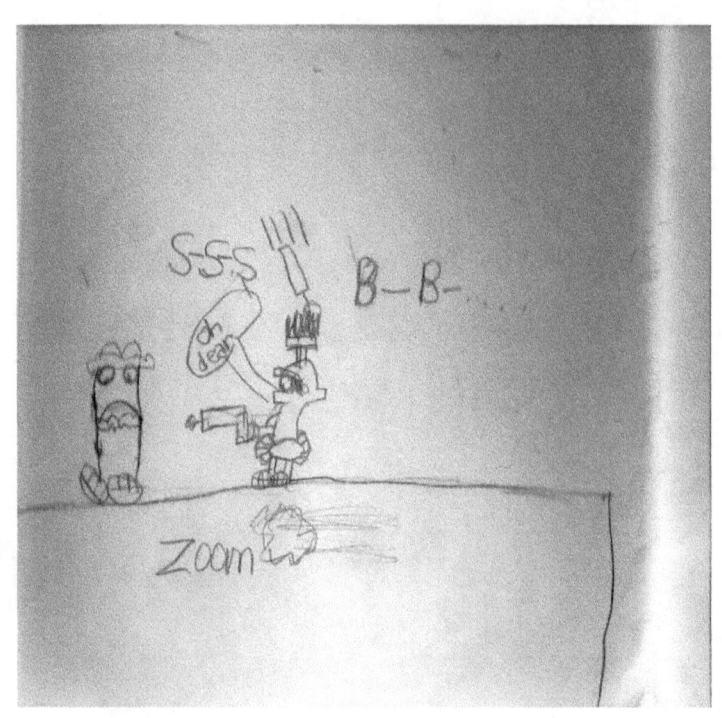

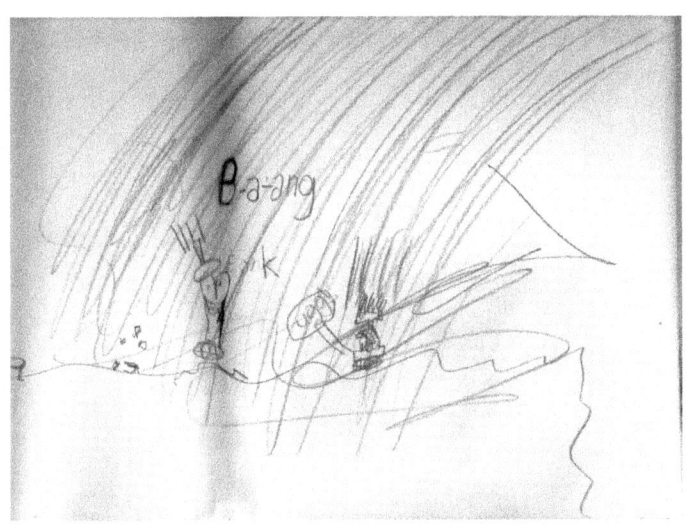

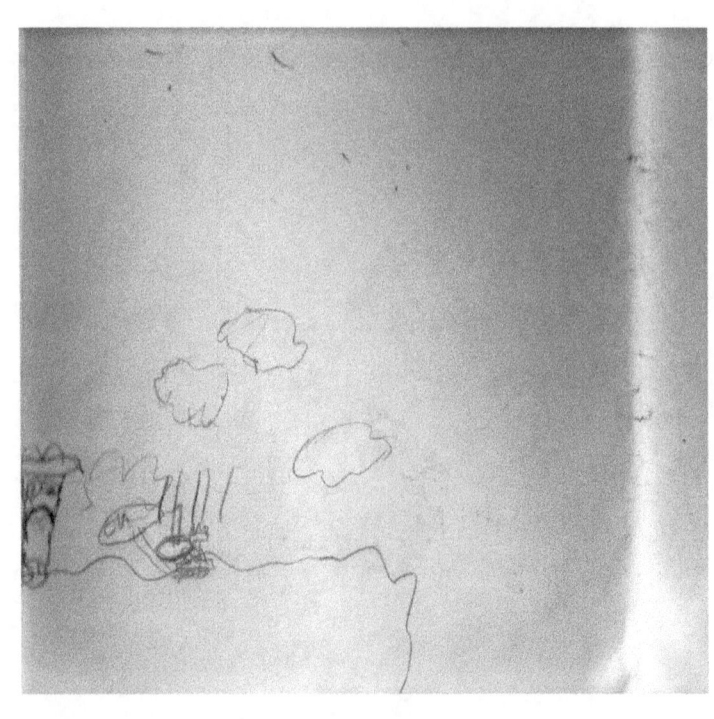

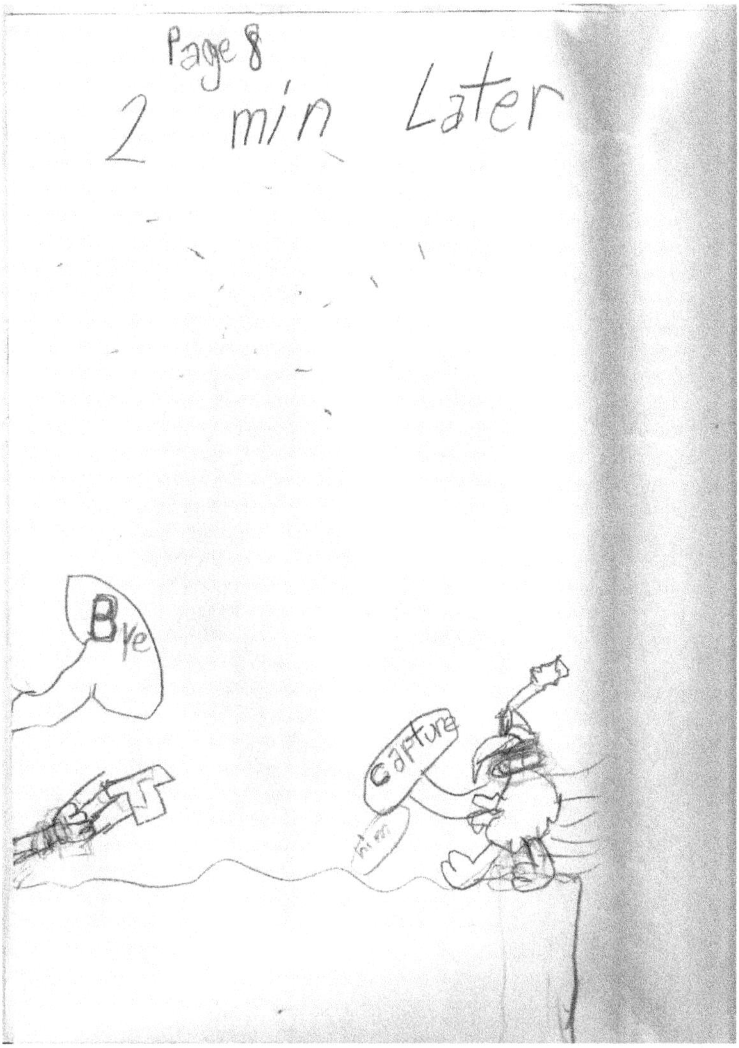
Page 8
2 min Later
Bye
capture
him

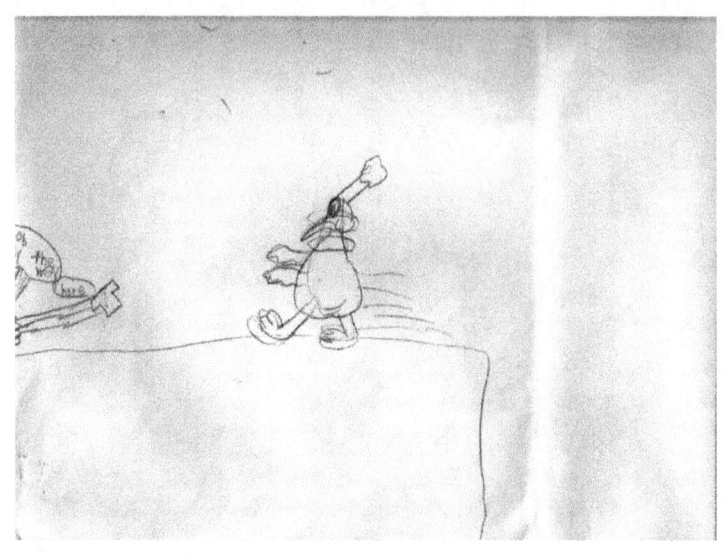

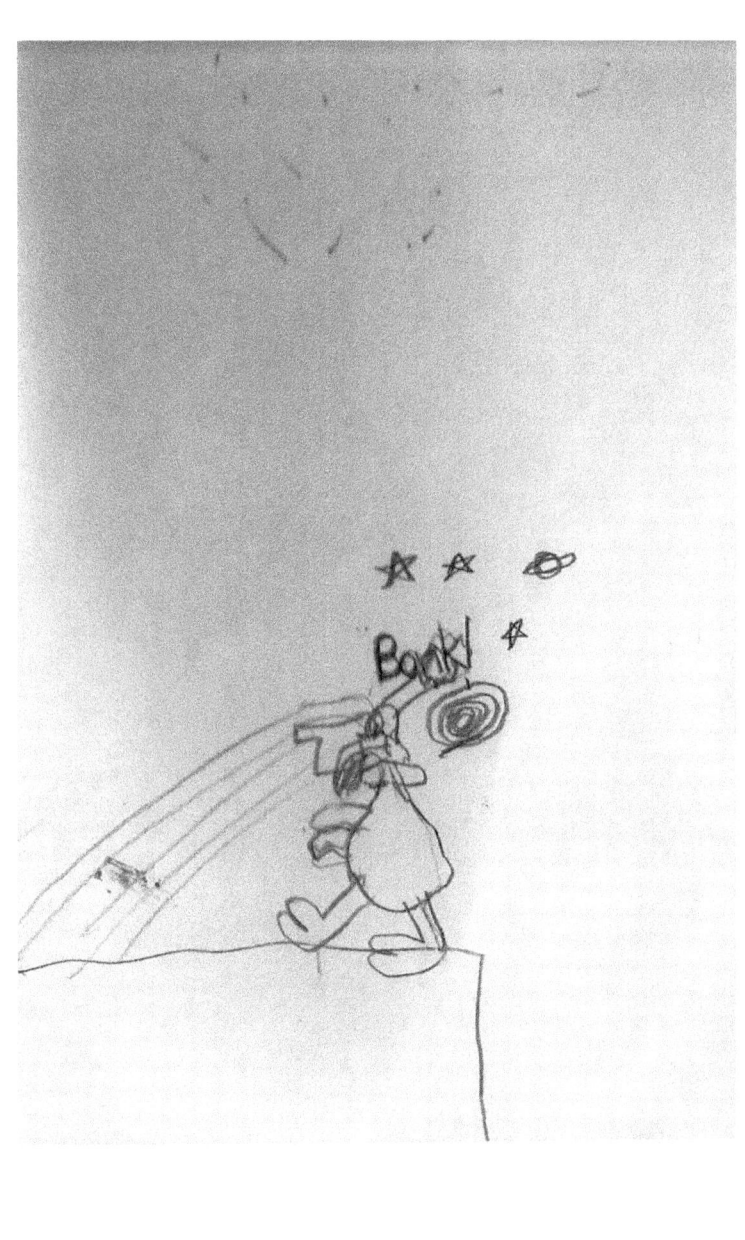

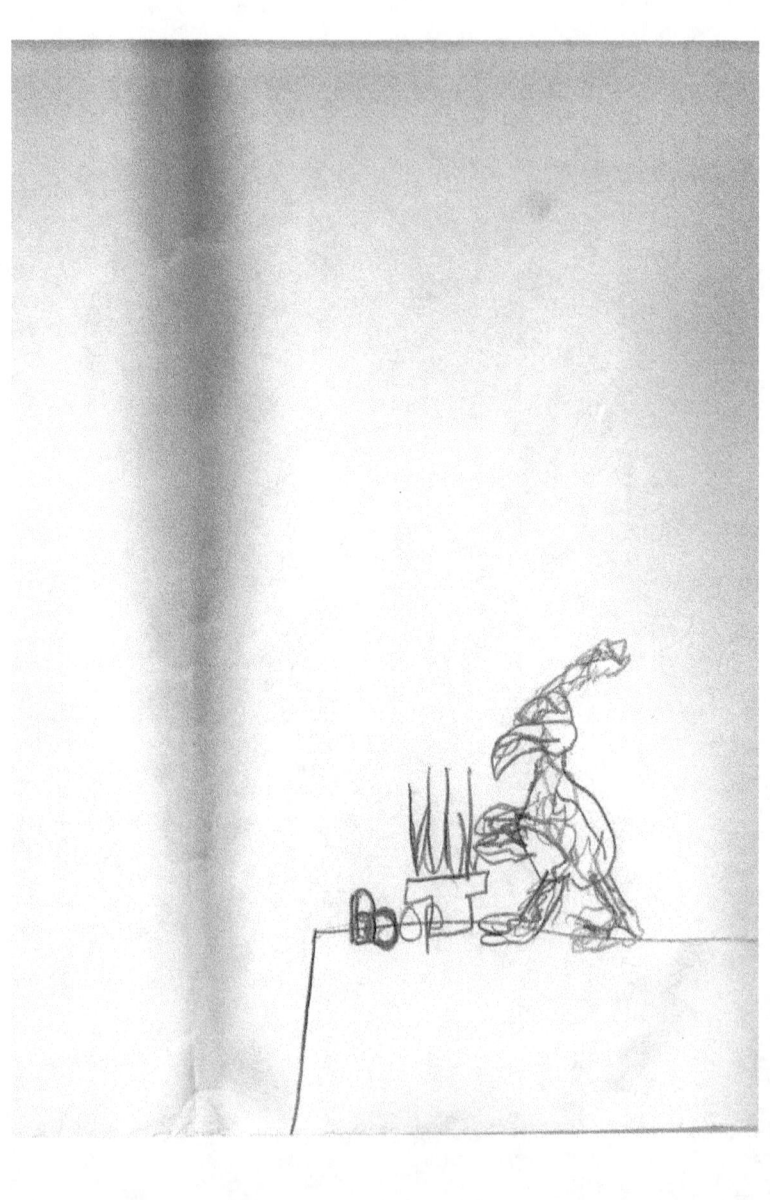

P. 12

$1\frac{3}{4}$ se

min   Later
P. 13

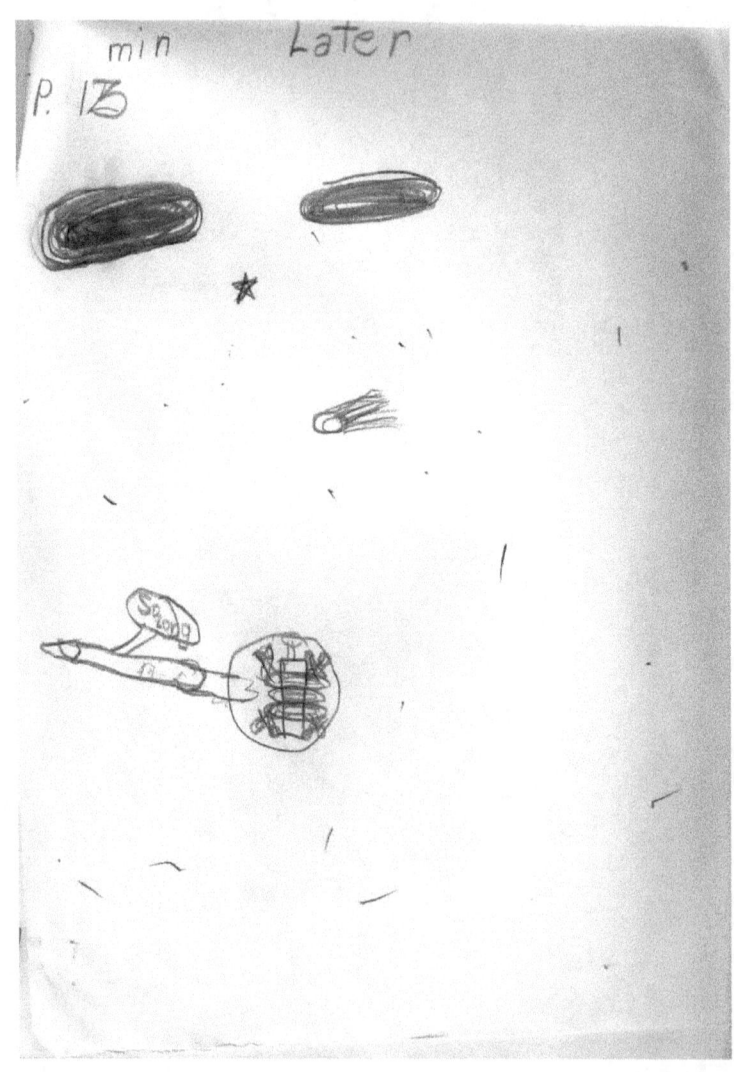

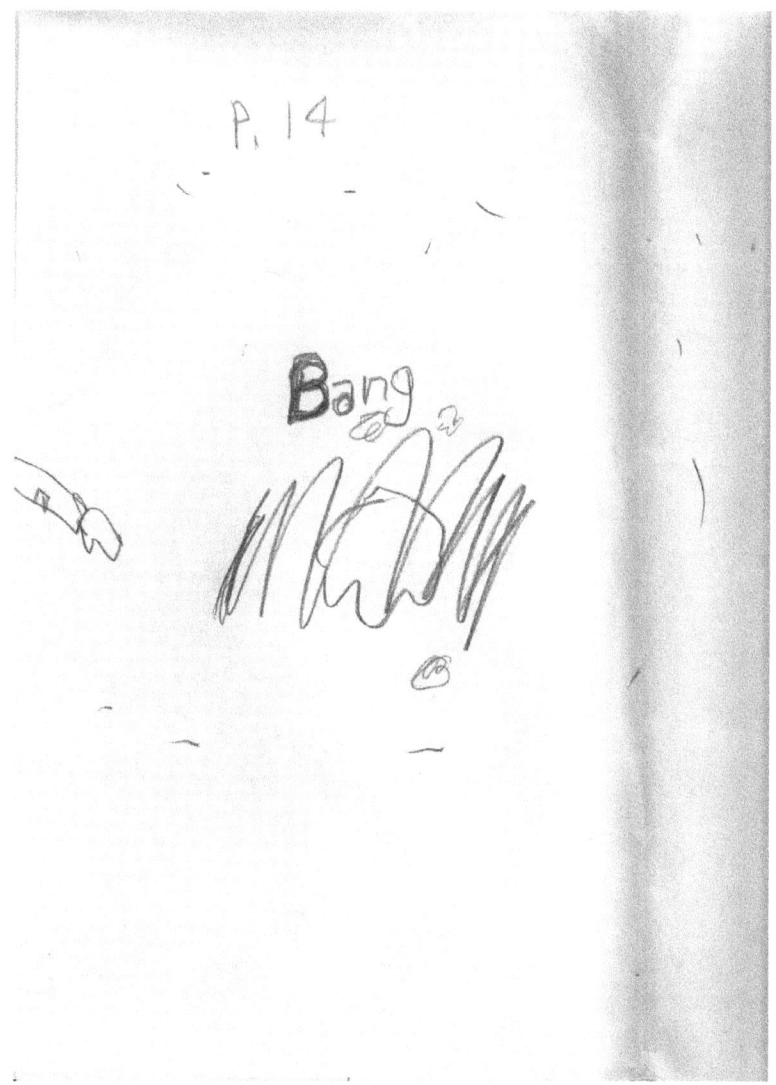

This cartoon was scanned completely all except for a small minscule moon off to the side of the picture.

— El Gato

City a continueaton of water well cartoon

We start off
with Daffy
spotting Speedy
and his friends
dyeing of thirst.
This time he helps
em.

Later Daffy is
investigating thesome
foot-points in
the desert on
his land he gets
off his camel
rushes to a city
and gets clobbed.

He says no one gets away with that and trys rockoling in it explodes.
He crawls under ground and gets clawed by 10 cats. He then rescues the mice lassoing in with a rifle.
Sylvester hands over his property. Speedy thanks him.
Daffy says after al smart mice are smart mice.
Sylvester says suffekin sucatash

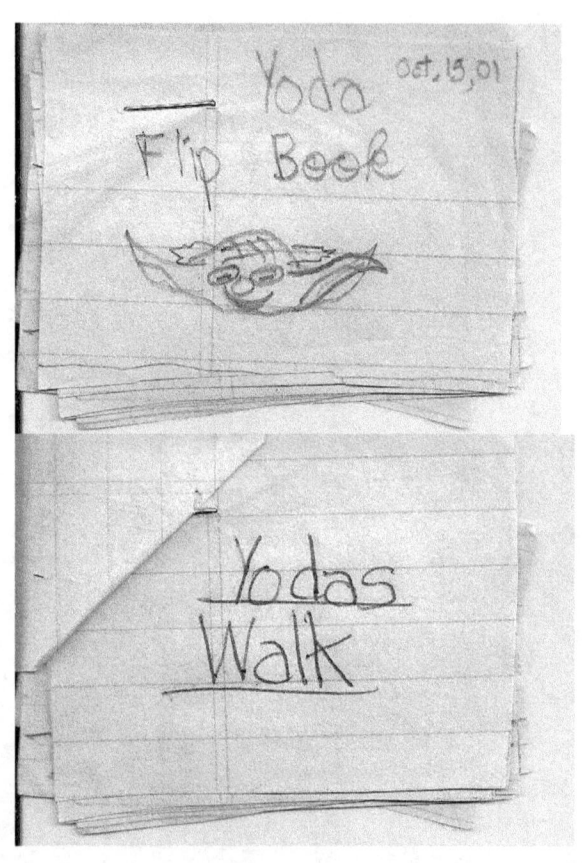

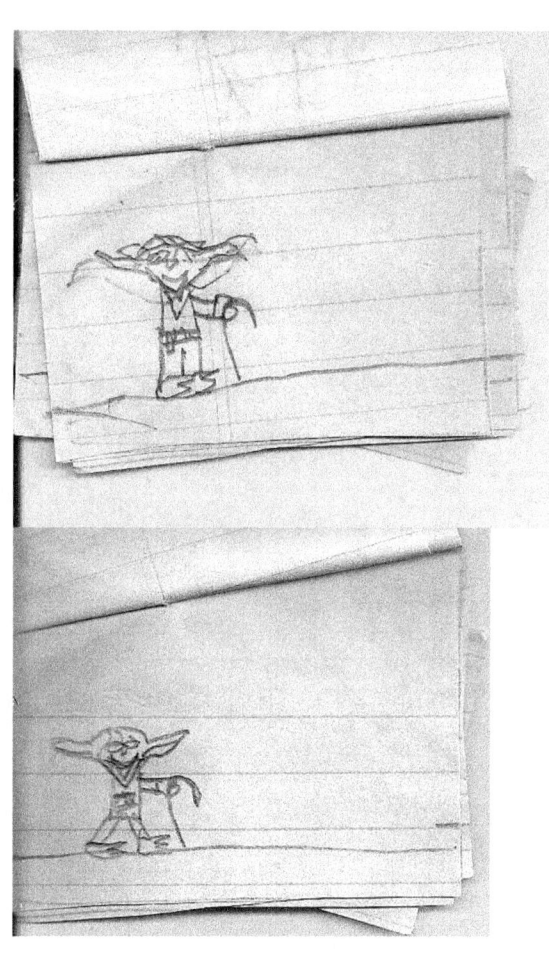

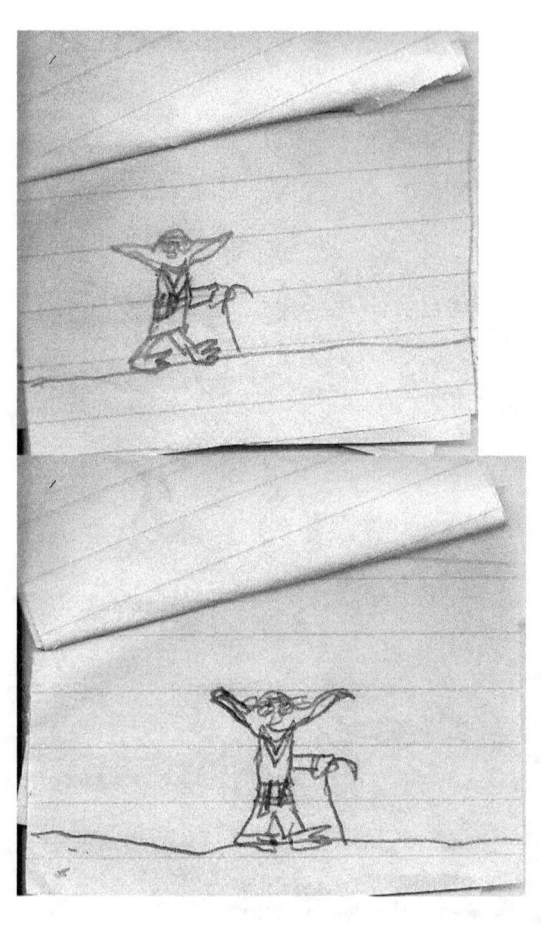

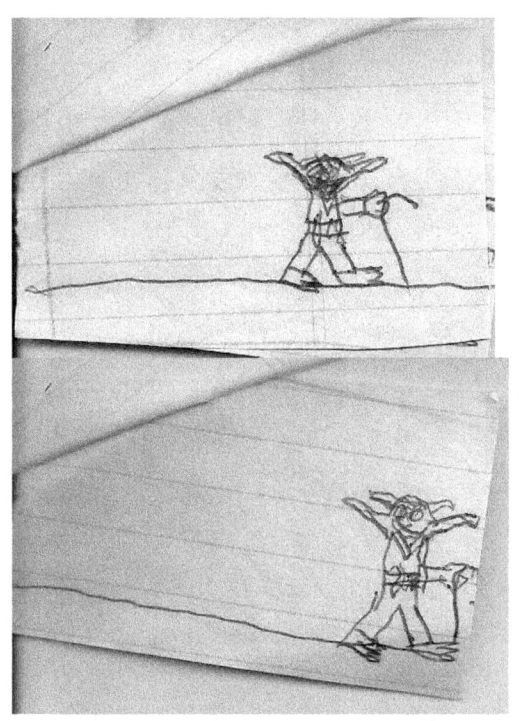

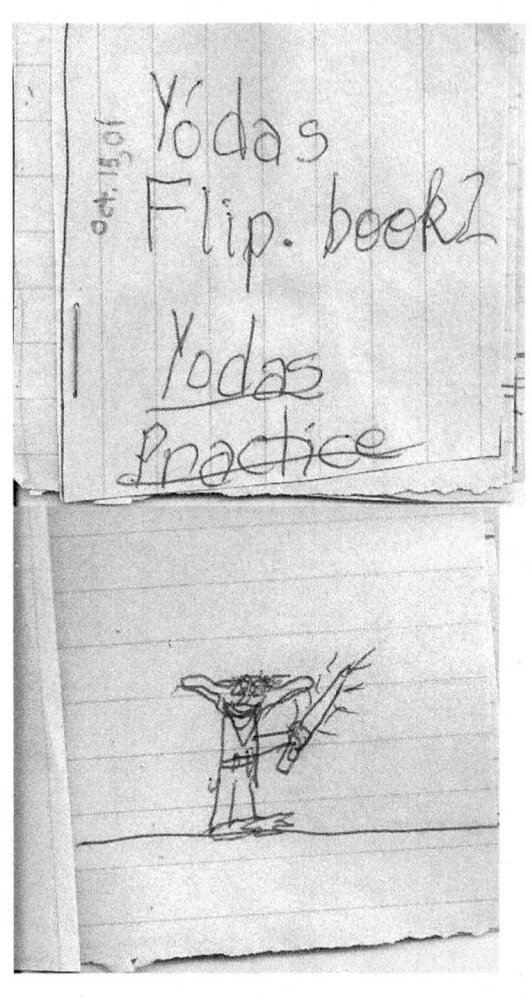

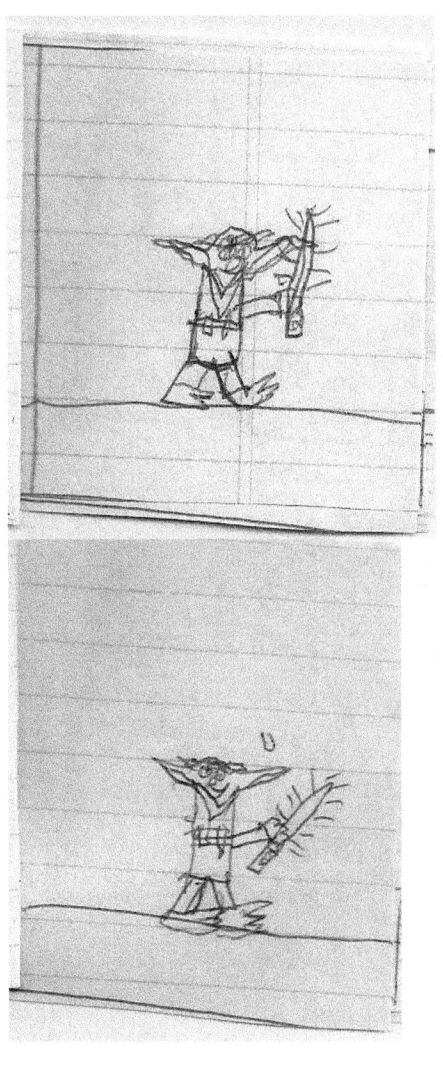

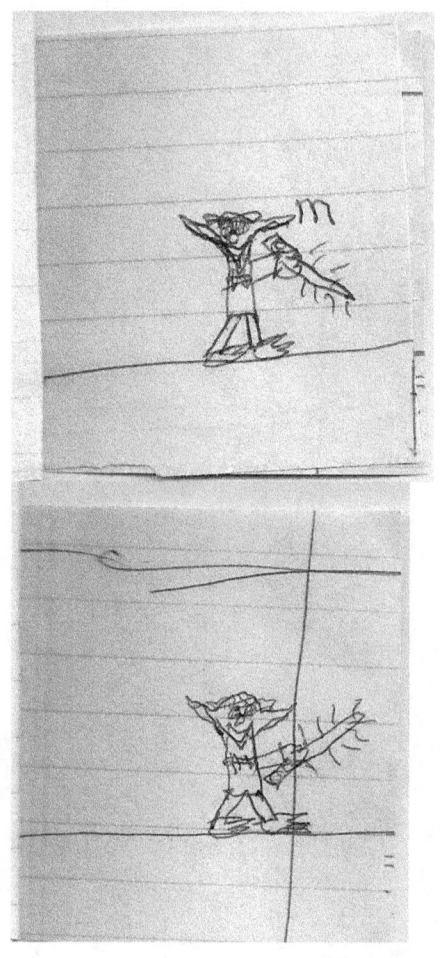

This book is done. Book 3 needs a lot of work still!

Need Amadalia flip, Smily and Munchy cartoon, other?

5 or eight other unscanned cartoons.